Sweet Things

Mug 'Ems make great gifts for your family and friends. Use the recipes in this book to assemble your homemade gift. Place the ingredients in a ziplock or food-safe bag and set the sealed bag in a decorative mug. Each recipe includes gift tags for your convenience – just cut them out, fold and personalize. Attach the personalized tag to the mug and decorate with ribbon, fabric and raffia.

When making these homemade gifts, use mugs that hold a volume of at least 1½ cups. For safety reasons, it is important that you do not give your gift in a metal or plastic mug.

Printed in the United States of America
by G&R Publishing Co.

Distributed By:

507 Industrial Street
Waverly, IA 50677

ISBN-13: 978-1-56383-199-7
ISBN-10: 1-56383-199-6
Item #3771

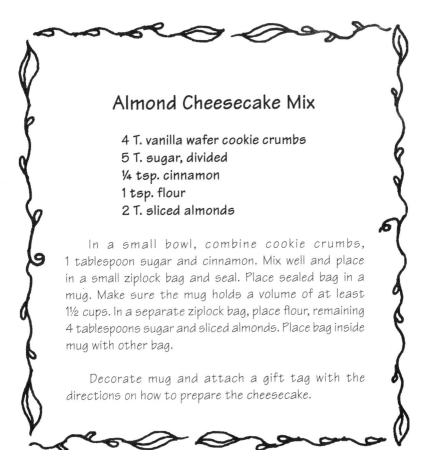

Almond Cheesecake Mix

4 T. vanilla wafer cookie crumbs
5 T. sugar, divided
¼ tsp. cinnamon
1 tsp. flour
2 T. sliced almonds

In a small bowl, combine cookie crumbs, 1 tablespoon sugar and cinnamon. Mix well and place in a small ziplock bag and seal. Place sealed bag in a mug. Make sure the mug holds a volume of at least 1½ cups. In a separate ziplock bag, place flour, remaining 4 tablespoons sugar and sliced almonds. Place bag inside mug with other bag.

Decorate mug and attach a gift tag with the directions on how to prepare the cheesecake.

Gift Tag Directions:
Almond Cheesecake

2 T. butter, melted
Almond Cheesecake Mix
4 oz. cream cheese, softened
1 egg yolk
½ tsp. almond extract
1 T. sour cream
1 T. whole milk or half n' half

Preheat oven to 350°. To make crust, in a small bowl, combine melted butter and contents of bag containing cookie crumbs. Mix well and press mixture into the bottom and halfway up sides of lightly greased mug. Bake in oven for 6 to 8 minutes. Meanwhile, in a separate bowl, combine contents of remaining bag, cream cheese, egg yolk, almond extract, sour cream and whole milk. Mix for 1 minute, until smooth. Allow crust to cool slightly and pour cream cheese mixture over crust in mug. Bake at 325° for 30 to 35 minutes. Enjoy!

Almond Cheesecake

2 T. butter, melted
Almond Cheesecake Mix
4 oz. cream cheese, softened
1 egg yolk
½ tsp. almond extract
1 T. sour cream
1 T. whole milk or half n' half

Preheat oven to 350°. To make crust, in a small bowl, combine melted butter and contents of bag containing cookie crumbs. Mix well and press mixture into the bottom and halfway up sides of lightly greased mug. Bake in oven for 6 to 8 minutes. Meanwhile, in a separate bowl, combine contents of remaining bag, cream cheese, egg yolk, almond extract, sour cream and whole milk. Mix for 1 minute, until smooth. Allow crust to cool slightly and pour cream cheese mixture over crust in mug. Bake at 325° for 30 to 35 minutes. Enjoy!

Almond Cheesecake

2 T. butter, melted
Almond Cheesecake Mix
4 oz. cream cheese, softened
1 egg yolk
½ tsp. almond extract
1 T. sour cream
1 T. whole milk or half n' half

Preheat oven to 350°. To make crust, in a small bowl, combine melted butter and contents of bag containing cookie crumbs. Mix well and press mixture into the bottom and halfway up sides of lightly greased mug. Bake in oven for 6 to 8 minutes. Meanwhile, in a separate bowl, combine contents of remaining bag, cream cheese, egg yolk, almond extract, sour cream and whole milk. Mix for 1 minute, until smooth. Allow crust to cool slightly and pour cream cheese mixture over crust in mug. Bake at 325° for 30 to 35 minutes. Enjoy!

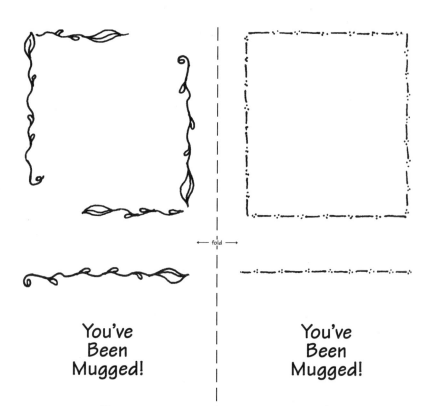

← fold →

You've
Been
Mugged!

MUG'EMS
by
CQ Products
www.cqproducts.com

You've
Been
Mugged!

MUG'EMS
by
CQ Products
www.cqproducts.com

Almond Cheesecake

2 T. butter, melted
Almond Cheesecake Mix
4 oz. cream cheese, softened
1 egg yolk
½ tsp. almond extract
1 T. sour cream
1 T. whole milk or half n' half

Preheat oven to 350°. To make crust, in a small bowl, combine melted butter and contents of bag containing cookie crumbs. Mix well and press mixture into the bottom and halfway up sides of lightly greased mug. Bake in oven for 6 to 8 minutes. Meanwhile, in a separate bowl, combine contents of remaining bag, cream cheese, egg yolk, almond extract, sour cream and whole milk. Mix for 1 minute, until smooth. Allow crust to cool slightly and pour cream cheese mixture over crust in mug. Bake at 325° for 30 to 35 minutes. Enjoy!

Almond Cheesecake

2 T. butter, melted
Almond Cheesecake Mix
4 oz. cream cheese, softened
1 egg yolk
½ tsp. almond extract
1 T. sour cream
1 T. whole milk or half n' half

Preheat oven to 350°. To make crust, in a small bowl, combine melted butter and contents of bag containing cookie crumbs. Mix well and press mixture into the bottom and halfway up sides of lightly greased mug. Bake in oven for 6 to 8 minutes. Meanwhile, in a separate bowl, combine contents of remaining bag, cream cheese, egg yolk, almond extract, sour cream and whole milk. Mix for 1 minute, until smooth. Allow crust to cool slightly and pour cream cheese mixture over crust in mug. Bake at 325° for 30 to 35 minutes. Enjoy!

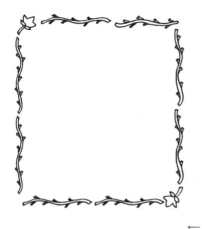

← fold →

You've
Been
Mugged!

You've
Been
Mugged!

MUG'EMS
by
CQ Products
www.cqproducts.com

MUG'EMS
by
CQ Products
www.cqproducts.com

Baked Custard Mix

2 T. sugar
1 tsp. cornstarch
1 T. currants
Pinch of nutmeg

In a small bowl, combine above ingredients. Mix well and place in a sandwich-size ziplock bag and seal. Place sealed bag in a mug. Make sure the mug holds a volume of at least 1½ cups.

Decorate mug and attach a gift tag with the directions on how to prepare the custard.

Gift Tag Directions:
Baked Custard

1 C. milk
Baked Custard Mix
½ tsp. vanilla
1 egg yolk, beaten

Preheat oven to 325°. In a medium saucepan over medium low heat, bring milk just to a simmer. In a medium bowl, combine Baked Custard Mix from bag with vanilla and beaten egg yolk. Mix thoroughly and add 1 tablespoon heated milk. Mix well and add mixture to saucepan with remaining milk. Mix thoroughly and pour mixture into mug. Bake in oven for 15 minutes. Enjoy!

Baked Custard

1 C. milk
Baked Custard Mix
½ tsp. vanilla
1 egg yolk, beaten

Preheat oven to 325°. In a medium saucepan over medium low heat, bring milk just to a simmer. In a medium bowl, combine Baked Custard Mix from bag with vanilla and beaten egg yolk. Mix thoroughly and add 1 tablespoon heated milk. Mix well and add mixture to saucepan with remaining milk. Mix thoroughly and pour mixture into mug. Bake in oven for 15 minutes. Enjoy!

Baked Custard

1 C. milk
Baked Custard Mix
½ tsp. vanilla
1 egg yolk, beaten

Preheat oven to 325°. In a medium saucepan over medium low heat, bring milk just to a simmer. In a medium bowl, combine Baked Custard Mix from bag with vanilla and beaten egg yolk. Mix thoroughly and add 1 tablespoon heated milk. Mix well and add mixture to saucepan with remaining milk. Mix thoroughly and pour mixture into mug. Bake in oven for 15 minutes. Enjoy!

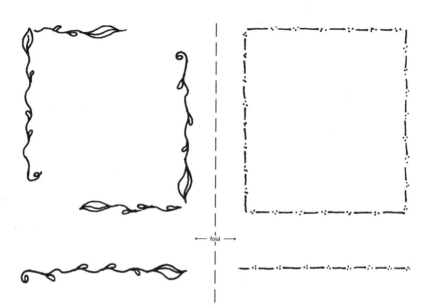

← fold →

You've
Been
Mugged!

MUG'EMS
by
CQ Products
www.cqproducts.com

You've
Been
Mugged!

MUG'EMS
by
CQ Products
www.cqproducts.com

Baked Custard

1 C. milk
Baked Custard Mix
½ tsp. vanilla
1 egg yolk, beaten

Preheat oven to 325°. In a medium saucepan over medium low heat, bring milk just to a simmer. In a medium bowl, combine Baked Custard Mix from bag with vanilla and beaten egg yolk. Mix thoroughly and add 1 tablespoon heated milk. Mix well and add mixture to saucepan with remaining milk. Mix thoroughly and pour mixture into mug. Bake in oven for 15 minutes. Enjoy!

Baked Custard

1 C. milk
Baked Custard Mix
½ tsp. vanilla
1 egg yolk, beaten

Preheat oven to 325°. In a medium saucepan over medium low heat, bring milk just to a simmer. In a medium bowl, combine Baked Custard Mix from bag with vanilla and beaten egg yolk. Mix thoroughly and add 1 tablespoon heated milk. Mix well and add mixture to saucepan with remaining milk. Mix thoroughly and pour mixture into mug. Bake in oven for 15 minutes. Enjoy!

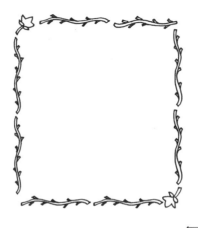

← fold →

You've
Been
Mugged!

You've
Been
Mugged!

MUG'EMS
by
CQ Products
www.cqproducts.com

MUG'EMS
by
CQ Products
www.cqproducts.com

Fudge Brownie Mix

3 T. brown sugar
¼ C. flour
¾ tsp. baking powder
⅛ tsp. salt
2 T. chopped walnuts or pecans

In a small bowl, combine above ingredients. Mix well and place in a sandwich-size ziplock bag and seal. Place sealed bag in a mug. Make sure the mug holds a volume of at least 1½ cups.

Decorate mug and attach a gift tag with the directions on how to prepare the brownie.

Gift Tag Directions:
Fudge Brownie

2 (1 oz.) squares unsweetened
    chocolate
1 T. butter
Fudge Brownie Mix
1 small egg
½ tsp. vanilla

Preheat oven to 350°. In a medium saucepan over
medium heat, combine unsweetened chocolate squares
and butter. Heat until mixture is melted and stir until
smooth. Remove from heat and let cool slightly. Add
Fudge Brownie mix from bag, egg and vanilla to melted
mixture and stir well. Pour mixture into lightly greased
mug. Bake in oven for 20 minutes. Enjoy!

Fudge Brownie

2 (1 oz.) squares
   unsweetened chocolate
1 T. butter
Fudge Brownie Mix
1 small egg
½ tsp. vanilla

   Preheat oven to 350°. In a medium saucepan over medium heat, combine unsweetened chocolate squares and butter. Heat until mixture is melted and stir until smooth. Remove from heat and let cool slightly. Add Fudge Brownie mix from bag, egg and vanilla to melted mixture and stir well. Pour mixture into lightly greased mug. Bake in oven for 20 minutes. Enjoy!

Fudge Brownie

2 (1 oz.) squares
   unsweetened chocolate
1 T. butter
Fudge Brownie Mix
1 small egg
½ tsp. vanilla

   Preheat oven to 350°. In a medium saucepan over medium heat, combine unsweetened chocolate squares and butter. Heat until mixture is melted and stir until smooth. Remove from heat and let cool slightly. Add Fudge Brownie mix from bag, egg and vanilla to melted mixture and stir well. Pour mixture into lightly greased mug. Bake in oven for 20 minutes. Enjoy!

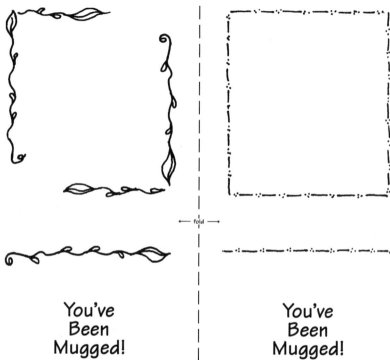

← fold →

You've
Been
Mugged!

MUG'EMS
by
CQ Products
www.cqproducts.com

You've
Been
Mugged!

MUG'EMS
by
CQ Products
www.cqproducts.com

Fudge Brownie

2 (1 oz.) squares
   unsweetened chocolate
1 T. butter
Fudge Brownie Mix
1 small egg
½ tsp. vanilla

Preheat oven to 350°. In a medium saucepan over medium heat, combine unsweetened chocolate squares and butter. Heat until mixture is melted and stir until smooth. Remove from heat and let cool slightly. Add Fudge Brownie mix from bag, egg and vanilla to melted mixture and stir well. Pour mixture into lightly greased mug. Bake in oven for 20 minutes. Enjoy!

Fudge Brownie

2 (1 oz.) squares
   unsweetened chocolate
1 T. butter
Fudge Brownie Mix
1 small egg
½ tsp. vanilla

Preheat oven to 350°. In a medium saucepan over medium heat, combine unsweetened chocolate squares and butter. Heat until mixture is melted and stir until smooth. Remove from heat and let cool slightly. Add Fudge Brownie mix from bag, egg and vanilla to melted mixture and stir well. Pour mixture into lightly greased mug. Bake in oven for 20 minutes. Enjoy!

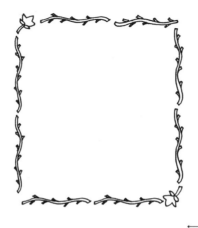

← fold →

You've
Been
Mugged!

You've
Been
Mugged!

MUG'EMS
by
CQ Products
www.cqproducts.com

MUG'EMS
by
CQ Products
www.cqproducts.com

Mocha Pudding Mix

¼ C. sugar
1 T. cocoa powder
1½ tsp. cornstarch
¾ tsp. instant coffee granules
⅛ tsp. salt

In a small bowl, combine above ingredients. Mix well and place in a sandwich-size ziplock bag and seal. Place sealed bag in a mug. Make sure the mug holds a volume of at least 1½ cups.

Decorate mug and attach a gift tag with the directions on how to prepare the pudding.

Gift Tag Directions:
Mocha Pudding

Mocha Pudding Mix
1 egg yolk
1 T. Kahlua liqueur, optional
1 C. whole milk

Pour Mocha Pudding Mix from bag into mug. Add egg yolk and Kahlua liqueur to ingredients in mug. Mix well and set aside. In a medium saucepan over medium heat, bring whole milk to a simmer. Add 1 tablespoon of pudding mixture from mug to saucepan and mix well. Pour milk mixture into mug with remaining pudding mixture and stir well. Place mug with pudding in microwave and heat for 1 minute, until pudding begins to thicken. Enjoy warm or chilled with a dollop of whipped topping!

Mocha Pudding

Mocha Pudding Mix
1 egg yolk
1 T. Kahlua liqueur, optional
1 C. whole milk

Pour Mocha Pudding Mix from bag into mug. Add egg yolk and Kahlua liqueur to ingredients in mug. Mix well and set aside. In a medium saucepan over medium heat, bring whole milk to a simmer. Add 1 tablespoon of pudding mixture from mug to saucepan and mix well. Pour milk mixture into mug with remaining pudding mixture and stir well. Place mug with pudding in microwave and heat for 1 minute, until pudding begins to thicken. Enjoy warm or chilled with a dollop of whipped topping!

Mocha Pudding

Mocha Pudding Mix
1 egg yolk
1 T. Kahlua liqueur, optional
1 C. whole milk

Pour Mocha Pudding Mix from bag into mug. Add egg yolk and Kahlua liqueur to ingredients in mug. Mix well and set aside. In a medium saucepan over medium heat, bring whole milk to a simmer. Add 1 tablespoon of pudding mixture from mug to saucepan and mix well. Pour milk mixture into mug with remaining pudding mixture and stir well. Place mug with pudding in microwave and heat for 1 minute, until pudding begins to thicken. Enjoy warm or chilled with a dollop of whipped topping!

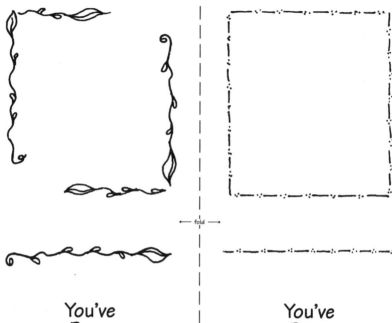

fold

You've
Been
Mugged!

You've
Been
Mugged!

MUG'EMS
by
CQ Products
www.cqproducts.com

MUG'EMS
by
CQ Products
www.cqproducts.com

Mocha Pudding

Mocha Pudding Mix
1 egg yolk
1 T. Kahlua liqueur, optional
1 C. whole milk

Pour Mocha Pudding Mix from bag into mug. Add egg yolk and Kahlua liqueur to ingredients in mug. Mix well and set aside. In a medium saucepan over medium heat, bring whole milk to a simmer. Add 1 tablespoon of pudding mixture from mug to saucepan and mix well. Pour milk mixture into mug with remaining pudding mixture and stir well. Place mug with pudding in microwave and heat for 1 minute, until pudding begins to thicken. Enjoy warm or chilled with a dollop of whipped topping!

Mocha Pudding

Mocha Pudding Mix
1 egg yolk
1 T. Kahlua liqueur, optional
1 C. whole milk

Pour Mocha Pudding Mix from bag into mug. Add egg yolk and Kahlua liqueur to ingredients in mug. Mix well and set aside. In a medium saucepan over medium heat, bring whole milk to a simmer. Add 1 tablespoon of pudding mixture from mug to saucepan and mix well. Pour milk mixture into mug with remaining pudding mixture and stir well. Place mug with pudding in microwave and heat for 1 minute, until pudding begins to thicken. Enjoy warm or chilled with a dollop of whipped topping!

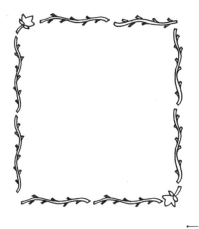

← fold →

You've
Been
Mugged!

MUG'EMS
by
CQ Products
www.cqproducts.com

You've
Been
Mugged!

MUG'EMS
by
CQ Products
www.cqproducts.com

Chocolate Chip Blondie Mix

3 T. brown sugar
4 T. flour
½ tsp. baking powder
⅛ tsp. salt
2 T. chopped pecans
2 T. miniature chocolate chips

In a small bowl, combine above ingredients. Mix well and place in a sandwich-size ziplock bag and seal. Place sealed bag in a mug. Make sure the mug holds a volume of at least 1½ cups.

Decorate mug and attach a gift tag with the directions on how to prepare the blondie.

Gift Tag Directions:
Chocolate Chip Blondie

2 T. margarine or butter
1 small egg
½ tsp. vanilla
Chocolate Chip Blondie Mix

Preheat oven to 350°. In a small microwave-safe bowl, place margarine. Heat in microwave until melted. Remove from microwave and let cool slightly. Stir in egg and vanilla. Add Chocolate Chip Blondie Mix from bag. Mix well until fully combined. Pour batter into lightly greased mug. Bake in oven for 17 to 19 minutes.

Chocolate Chip Blondie

2 T. margarine or butter
1 small egg
½ tsp. vanilla
Chocolate Chip Blondie Mix

Preheat oven to 350°. In a small microwave-safe bowl, place margarine. Heat in microwave until melted. Remove from microwave and let cool slightly. Stir in egg and vanilla. Add Chocolate Chip Blondie Mix from bag. Mix well until fully combined. Pour batter into lightly greased mug. Bake in oven for 17 to 19 minutes.

Chocolate Chip Blondie

2 T. margarine or butter
1 small egg
½ tsp. vanilla
Chocolate Chip Blondie Mix

Preheat oven to 350°. In a small microwave-safe bowl, place margarine. Heat in microwave until melted. Remove from microwave and let cool slightly. Stir in egg and vanilla. Add Chocolate Chip Blondie Mix from bag. Mix well until fully combined. Pour batter into lightly greased mug. Bake in oven for 17 to 19 minutes.

← fold →

You've
Been
Mugged!

MUG'EMS
by
CQ Products
www.cqproducts.com

You've
Been
Mugged!

MUG'EMS
by
CQ Products
www.cqproducts.com

Chocolate Chip Blondie

2 T. margarine or butter
1 small egg
½ tsp. vanilla
Chocolate Chip Blondie Mix

Preheat oven to 350°. In a small microwave-safe bowl, place margarine. Heat in microwave until melted. Remove from microwave and let cool slightly. Stir in egg and vanilla. Add Chocolate Chip Blondie Mix from bag. Mix well until fully combined. Pour batter into lightly greased mug. Bake in oven for 17 to 19 minutes.

Chocolate Chip Blondie

2 T. margarine or butter
1 small egg
½ tsp. vanilla
Chocolate Chip Blondie Mix

Preheat oven to 350°. In a small microwave-safe bowl, place margarine. Heat in microwave until melted. Remove from microwave and let cool slightly. Stir in egg and vanilla. Add Chocolate Chip Blondie Mix from bag. Mix well until fully combined. Pour batter into lightly greased mug. Bake in oven for 17 to 19 minutes.

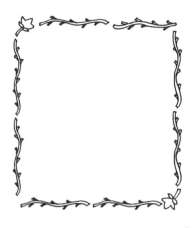

← fold →

You've
Been
Mugged!

You've
Been
Mugged!

MUG'EMS
by
CQ Products
www.cqproducts.com

MUG'EMS
by
CQ Products
www.cqproducts.com

Rice Pudding Mix

2 T. sugar
Pinch of salt
2 T. instant rice
2 T. raisins
Pinch of cinnamon

In a small bowl, combine above ingredients. Mix well and place in a sandwich-size ziplock bag and seal. Place sealed bag in a mug. Make sure the mug holds a volume of at least 1½ cups.

Decorate mug and attach a gift tag with the directions on how to prepare the pudding.

Gift Tag Directions:
Rice Pudding

Rice Pudding Mix
1 C. milk
1 small egg, beaten
1 tsp. vanilla

Preheat oven to 300°. In a small bowl, place Rice Pudding Mix from bag. In a small saucepan over medium heat, bring milk to a simmer. Pour simmering milk over mix in bowl. Cover bowl and let sit for 5 minutes. Stir in beaten egg and vanilla. Pour mixture into mug. Cover mug with foil and bake in oven for 15 to 20 minutes. Enjoy!

Rice Pudding

Rice Pudding Mix
1 C. milk
1 small egg, beaten
1 tsp. vanilla

Preheat oven to 300°. In a small bowl, place Rice Pudding Mix from bag. In a small saucepan over medium heat, bring milk to a simmer. Pour simmering milk over mix in bowl. Cover bowl and let sit for 5 minutes. Stir in beaten egg and vanilla. Pour mixture into mug. Cover mug with foil and bake in oven for 15 to 20 minutes. Enjoy!

Rice Pudding

Rice Pudding Mix
1 C. milk
1 small egg, beaten
1 tsp. vanilla

Preheat oven to 300°. In a small bowl, place Rice Pudding Mix from bag. In a small saucepan over medium heat, bring milk to a simmer. Pour simmering milk over mix in bowl. Cover bowl and let sit for 5 minutes. Stir in beaten egg and vanilla. Pour mixture into mug. Cover mug with foil and bake in oven for 15 to 20 minutes. Enjoy!

fold

You've
Been
Mugged!

You've
Been
Mugged!

MUG'EMS
by
CQ Products
www.cqproducts.com

MUG'EMS
by
CQ Products
www.cqproducts.com

Rice Pudding

Rice Pudding Mix
1 C. milk
1 small egg, beaten
1 tsp. vanilla

Preheat oven to 300°. In a small bowl, place Rice Pudding Mix from bag. In a small saucepan over medium heat, bring milk to a simmer. Pour simmering milk over mix in bowl. Cover bowl and let sit for 5 minutes. Stir in beaten egg and vanilla. Pour mixture into mug. Cover mug with foil and bake in oven for 15 to 20 minutes. Enjoy!

Rice Pudding

Rice Pudding Mix
1 C. milk
1 small egg, beaten
1 tsp. vanilla

Preheat oven to 300°. In a small bowl, place Rice Pudding Mix from bag. In a small saucepan over medium heat, bring milk to a simmer. Pour simmering milk over mix in bowl. Cover bowl and let sit for 5 minutes. Stir in beaten egg and vanilla. Pour mixture into mug. Cover mug with foil and bake in oven for 15 to 20 minutes. Enjoy!

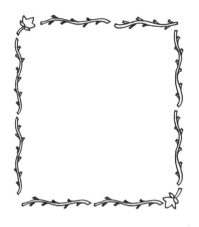

← fold →

You've
Been
Mugged!

You've
Been
Mugged!

MUG'EMS
by
CQ Products
www.cqproducts.com

MUG'EMS
by
CQ Products
www.cqproducts.com

Shoofly Pie Mix

5 T. flour
2 T. dark brown sugar
¼ tsp. cinnamon
Pinch of salt
Pinch of nutmeg
Pinch of ground ginger

In a small bowl, combine above ingredients. Mix well and place in a sandwich-size ziplock bag and seal. Place sealed bag in a mug. Make sure the mug holds a volume of at least 1½ cups.

Decorate mug and attach a gift tag with the directions on how to prepare the pie.

Gift Tag Directions:
Shoofly Pie

Shoofly Pie Mix
3 T. shortening, butter or margarine
2 T. water
2 T. molasses
1 tsp. baking soda

Preheat oven to 350°. In a small bowl, place Shoofly Pie Mix from bag. Using a pastry blender, cut in shortening until mixture resembles fine crumbs. Press ¼ of the mixture into bottom and halfway up sides of lightly greased mug. Bake in oven for 6 to 10 minutes. Place water in a glass bowl and microwave until just boiling. Stir in molasses and baking soda. To assemble pie, alternate layers of ⅓ of the remaining crumb mixture, followed by ½ of the molasses mixture. Layer another ⅓ of the crumb mixture followed by remaining molasses mixture. Top with final ⅓ of the crumb mixture. Bake in oven for 15 to 20 minutes. Enjoy!

Shoofly Pie

Shoofly Pie Mix
3 T. shortening, butter
   or margarine
2 T. water
2 T. molasses
1 tsp. baking soda

Preheat oven to 350°. In a small bowl, place Shoofly Pie Mix from bag. Using a pastry blender, cut in shortening until mixture resembles fine crumbs. Press ¼ of the mixture into bottom and halfway up sides of lightly greased mug. Bake in oven for 6 to 10 minutes. Place water in a glass bowl and microwave until just boiling. Stir in molasses and baking soda. To assemble pie, alternate layers of ⅓ of the remaining crumb mixture, followed by ½ of the molasses mixture. Layer another ⅓ of the crumb mixture followed by remaining molasses mixture. Top with final ⅓ of the crumb mixture. Bake in oven for 15 to 20 minutes. Enjoy!

Shoofly Pie

Shoofly Pie Mix
3 T. shortening, butter
   or margarine
2 T. water
2 T. molasses
1 tsp. baking soda

Preheat oven to 350°. In a small bowl, place Shoofly Pie Mix from bag. Using a pastry blender, cut in shortening until mixture resembles fine crumbs. Press ¼ of the mixture into bottom and halfway up sides of lightly greased mug. Bake in oven for 6 to 10 minutes. Place water in a glass bowl and microwave until just boiling. Stir in molasses and baking soda. To assemble pie, alternate layers of ⅓ of the remaining crumb mixture, followed by ½ of the molasses mixture. Layer another ⅓ of the crumb mixture followed by remaining molasses mixture. Top with final ⅓ of the crumb mixture. Bake in oven for 15 to 20 minutes. Enjoy!

← fold →

You've
Been
Mugged!

MUG'EMS
by
CQ Products
www.cqproducts.com

You've
Been
Mugged!

MUG'EMS
by
CQ Products
www.cqproducts.com

Shoofly Pie

Shoofly Pie Mix
3 T. shortening, butter
   or margarine
2 T. water
2 T. molasses
1 tsp. baking soda

Preheat oven to 350°. In a small bowl, place Shoofly Pie Mix from bag. Using a pastry blender, cut in shortening until mixture resembles fine crumbs. Press ¼ of the mixture into bottom and halfway up sides of lightly greased mug. Bake in oven for 6 to 10 minutes. Place water in a glass bowl and microwave until just boiling. Stir in molasses and baking soda. To assemble pie, alternate layers of ⅓ of the remaining crumb mixture, followed by ½ of the molasses mixture. Layer another ⅓ of the crumb mixture followed by remaining molasses mixture. Top with final ⅓ of the crumb mixture. Bake in oven for 15 to 20 minutes. Enjoy!

Shoofly Pie

Shoofly Pie Mix
3 T. shortening, butter
   or margarine
2 T. water
2 T. molasses
1 tsp. baking soda

Preheat oven to 350°. In a small bowl, place Shoofly Pie Mix from bag. Using a pastry blender, cut in shortening until mixture resembles fine crumbs. Press ¼ of the mixture into bottom and halfway up sides of lightly greased mug. Bake in oven for 6 to 10 minutes. Place water in a glass bowl and microwave until just boiling. Stir in molasses and baking soda. To assemble pie, alternate layers of ⅓ of the remaining crumb mixture, followed by ½ of the molasses mixture. Layer another ⅓ of the crumb mixture followed by remaining molasses mixture. Top with final ⅓ of the crumb mixture. Bake in oven for 15 to 20 minutes. Enjoy!

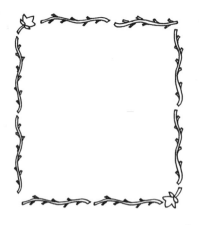

← fold →

You've
Been
Mugged!

You've
Been
Mugged!

MUG'EMS
by
CQ Products
www.cqproducts.com

MUG'EMS
by
CQ Products
www.cqproducts.com

Apple Crisp Mix

3 T. sugar
2½ T. flour, divided
½ tsp. cinnamon, divided
4 T. old fashioned oats
3 T. brown sugar

In a small bowl, combine sugar, 1 tablespoon flour and ¼ teaspoon cinnamon. Mix well and place in a small ziplock bag and seal. Place sealed bag in a mug. Make sure the mug holds a volume of at least 1½ cups. In a separate ziplock bag, place old fashioned oats, brown sugar, remaining 1½ tablespoons flour and remaining ¼ teaspoon cinnamon. Place bag inside mug with other bag.

Decorate mug and attach a gift tag with the directions on how to prepare the apple crisp.

Gift Tag Directions:
Apple Crisp

1 small apple
Apple Crisp Mix
3 T. butter, melted

Preheat oven to 350°. Peel, core and chop apple into pieces. In a small bowl, place contents of bag containing the sugar mix. Add chopped apples and toss until evenly coated. Place apple mixture in lightly greased mug. In a separate bowl, place contents of bag containing the oats mixture. Pour melted butter over mixture and stir well. Crumble oats mixture over apple mixture in mug. Bake in oven for 20 to 25 minutes. Enjoy!

Apple Crisp

1 small apple
Apple Crisp Mix
3 T. butter, melted

   Preheat oven to 350°. Peel, core and chop apple into pieces. In a small bowl, place contents of bag containing the sugar mix. Add chopped apples and toss until evenly coated. Place apple mixture in lightly greased mug. In a separate bowl, place contents of bag containing the oats mixture. Pour melted butter over mixture and stir well. Crumble oats mixture over apple mixture in mug. Bake in oven for 20 to 25 minutes. Enjoy!

Apple Crisp

1 small apple
Apple Crisp Mix
3 T. butter, melted

   Preheat oven to 350°. Peel, core and chop apple into pieces. In a small bowl, place contents of bag containing the sugar mix. Add chopped apples and toss until evenly coated. Place apple mixture in lightly greased mug. In a separate bowl, place contents of bag containing the oats mixture. Pour melted butter over mixture and stir well. Crumble oats mixture over apple mixture in mug. Bake in oven for 20 to 25 minutes. Enjoy!

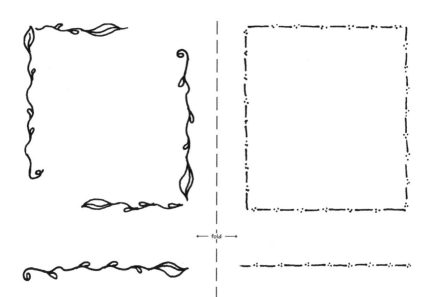

← fold →

You've
Been
Mugged!

You've
Been
Mugged!

MUG'EMS
by
CQ Products
www.cqproducts.com

MUG'EMS
by
CQ Products
www.cqproducts.com

Apple Crisp

1 small apple
Apple Crisp Mix
3 T. butter, melted

Preheat oven to 350°. Peel, core and chop apple into pieces. In a small bowl, place contents of bag containing the sugar mix. Add chopped apples and toss until evenly coated. Place apple mixture in lightly greased mug. In a separate bowl, place contents of bag containing the oats mixture. Pour melted butter over mixture and stir well. Crumble oats mixture over apple mixture in mug. Bake in oven for 20 to 25 minutes. Enjoy!

Apple Crisp

1 small apple
Apple Crisp Mix
3 T. butter, melted

Preheat oven to 350°. Peel, core and chop apple into pieces. In a small bowl, place contents of bag containing the sugar mix. Add chopped apples and toss until evenly coated. Place apple mixture in lightly greased mug. In a separate bowl, place contents of bag containing the oats mixture. Pour melted butter over mixture and stir well. Crumble oats mixture over apple mixture in mug. Bake in oven for 20 to 25 minutes. Enjoy!

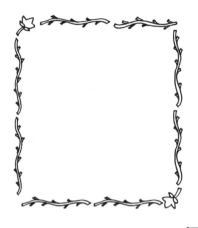

← fold →

You've
Been
Mugged!

MUG'EMS
by
CQ Products
www.cqproducts.com

You've
Been
Mugged!

MUG'EMS
by
CQ Products
www.cqproducts.com

Chocolate Cakelette Mix

4 T. flour
3 T. sugar
1 T. cocoa powder
¾ tsp. baking powder
2 T. miniature chocolate chips

In a small bowl, combine above ingredients. Mix well and place in a sandwich-size ziplock bag and seal. Place sealed bag in a mug. Make sure the mug holds a volume of at least 1½ cups.

Decorate mug and attach a gift tag with the directions on how to prepare the cakelette.

Gift Tag Directions:
Chocolate Cakelette

3 T. water
1 small egg
2 T. vegetable oil
½ tsp. vanilla
Chocolate Cakelette Mix

Preheat oven to 350°. In a small bowl, combine water, egg, vegetable oil and vanilla. Mix well and add Chocolate Cakelette Mix from bag. Stir until well combined. Spoon batter into lightly greased mug. Bake in oven for 15 to 20 minutes. Enjoy!

Chocolate Cakelette

3 T. water
1 small egg
2 T. vegetable oil
½ tsp. vanilla
Chocolate Cakelette Mix

Preheat oven to 350°. In a small bowl, combine water, egg, vegetable oil and vanilla. Mix well and add Chocolate Cakelette Mix from bag. Stir until well combined. Spoon batter into lightly greased mug. Bake in oven for 15 to 20 minutes. Enjoy!

Chocolate Cakelette

3 T. water
1 small egg
2 T. vegetable oil
½ tsp. vanilla
Chocolate Cakelette Mix

Preheat oven to 350°. In a small bowl, combine water, egg, vegetable oil and vanilla. Mix well and add Chocolate Cakelette Mix from bag. Stir until well combined. Spoon batter into lightly greased mug. Bake in oven for 15 to 20 minutes. Enjoy!

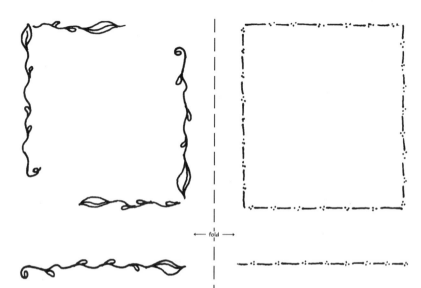

← fold →

You've
Been
Mugged!

MUG'EMS
by
CQ Products
www.cqproducts.com

You've
Been
Mugged!

MUG'EMS
by
CQ Products
www.cqproducts.com

Chocolate Cakelette

3 T. water
1 small egg
2 T. vegetable oil
½ tsp. vanilla
Chocolate Cakelette Mix

Preheat oven to 350°. In a small bowl, combine water, egg, vegetable oil and vanilla. Mix well and add Chocolate Cakelette Mix from bag. Stir until well combined. Spoon batter into lightly greased mug. Bake in oven for 15 to 20 minutes. Enjoy!

Chocolate Cakelette

3 T. water
1 small egg
2 T. vegetable oil
½ tsp. vanilla
Chocolate Cakelette Mix

Preheat oven to 350°. In a small bowl, combine water, egg, vegetable oil and vanilla. Mix well and add Chocolate Cakelette Mix from bag. Stir until well combined. Spoon batter into lightly greased mug. Bake in oven for 15 to 20 minutes. Enjoy!

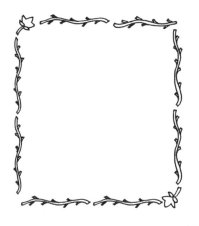

← fold →

You've
Been
Mugged!

You've
Been
Mugged!

MUG'EMS
by
CQ Products
www.cqproducts.com

MUG'EMS
by
CQ Products
www.cqproducts.com

Bread Pudding Mix

2 T. raisins
3 T. sugar
1 C. French bread cubes

In a small bowl, combine above ingredients. Mix well and place in a sandwich-size ziplock bag and seal. Place sealed bag in a mug. Make sure the mug holds a volume of at least 1½ cups.

Decorate mug and attach a gift tag with the directions on how to prepare the bread pudding.

Gift Tag Directions:
Bread Pudding

Bread Pudding Mix
1 T. butter or margarine, melted
1 small egg
1 C. milk
1 tsp. vanilla

Preheat oven to 325°. Pour Bread Pudding Mix from bag into mug. In a small bowl, combine melted butter, egg, milk and vanilla. Mix well. Pour butter mixture over ingredients in mug. Do not mix. Bake in oven for 25 minutes. Enjoy!

Bread Pudding

Bread Pudding Mix
1 T. butter or margarine, melted
1 small egg
1 C. milk
1 tsp. vanilla

Preheat oven to 325°. Pour Bread Pudding Mix from bag into mug. In a small bowl, combine melted butter, egg, milk and vanilla. Mix well. Pour butter mixture over ingredients in mug. Do not mix. Bake in oven for 25 minutes. Enjoy!

Bread Pudding

Bread Pudding Mix
1 T. butter or margarine, melted
1 small egg
1 C. milk
1 tsp. vanilla

Preheat oven to 325°. Pour Bread Pudding Mix from bag into mug. In a small bowl, combine melted butter, egg, milk and vanilla. Mix well. Pour butter mixture over ingredients in mug. Do not mix. Bake in oven for 25 minutes. Enjoy!

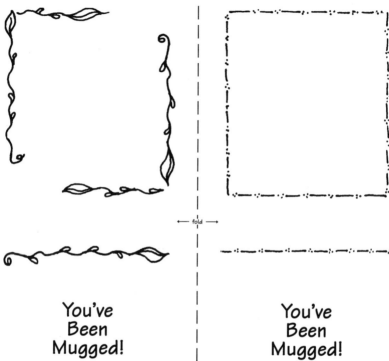

← fold →

You've
Been
Mugged!

MUG'EMS
by
CQ Products
www.cqproducts.com

You've
Been
Mugged!

MUG'EMS
by
CQ Products
www.cqproducts.com

Bread Pudding

Bread Pudding Mix
1 T. butter or margarine, melted
1 small egg
1 C. milk
1 tsp. vanilla

Preheat oven to 325°. Pour Bread Pudding Mix from bag into mug. In a small bowl, combine melted butter, egg, milk and vanilla. Mix well. Pour butter mixture over ingredients in mug. Do not mix. Bake in oven for 25 minutes. Enjoy!

Bread Pudding

Bread Pudding Mix
1 T. butter or margarine, melted
1 small egg
1 C. milk
1 tsp. vanilla

Preheat oven to 325°. Pour Bread Pudding Mix from bag into mug. In a small bowl, combine melted butter, egg, milk and vanilla. Mix well. Pour butter mixture over ingredients in mug. Do not mix. Bake in oven for 25 minutes. Enjoy!

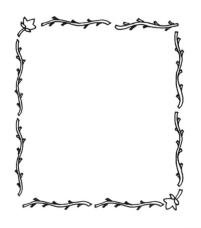

← fold →

You've
Been
Mugged!

You've
Been
Mugged!

MUG'EMS
by
CQ Products
www.cqproducts.com

MUG'EMS
by
CQ Products
www.cqproducts.com

Carrot Cake Mix

4 T. flour
2 T. sugar
1 T. brown sugar
¼ tsp. cinnamon
Pinch of nutmeg
Pinch of ground cloves
¾ tsp. baking powder
1 T. shredded coconut
1 T. chopped walnuts
1 T. golden raisins

In a small bowl, combine above ingredients. Mix well and place in a sandwich-size ziplock bag and seal. Place sealed bag in a mug. Make sure the mug holds a volume of at least 1½ cups.

Decorate mug and attach a gift tag with the directions on how to prepare the cake.

Gift Tag Directions:
Carrot Cake

Carrot Cake Mix
1 small egg
1 T. vegetable oil
2 T. orange juice with pulp
2 T. shredded carrots

Preheat oven to 350°. In a small bowl, place Carrot Cake Mix from bag. Add egg, vegetable oil, orange juice and shredded carrots and mix until well combined. Pour mixture into lightly greased mug. Bake in oven for 20 minutes. Enjoy!

Carrot Cake

Carrot Cake Mix
1 small egg
1 T. vegetable oil
2 T. orange juice with pulp
2 T. shredded carrots

   Preheat oven to 350°. In a small bowl, place Carrot Cake Mix from bag. Add egg, vegetable oil, orange juice and shredded carrots and mix until well combined. Pour mixture into lightly greased mug. Bake in oven for 20 minutes. Enjoy!

Carrot Cake

Carrot Cake Mix
1 small egg
1 T. vegetable oil
2 T. orange juice with pulp
2 T. shredded carrots

   Preheat oven to 350°. In a small bowl, place Carrot Cake Mix from bag. Add egg, vegetable oil, orange juice and shredded carrots and mix until well combined. Pour mixture into lightly greased mug. Bake in oven for 20 minutes. Enjoy!

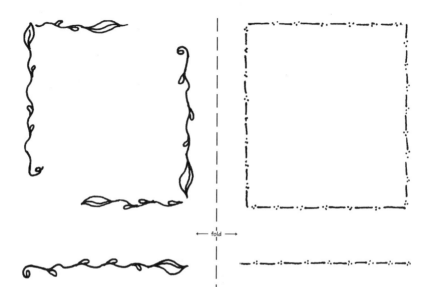

← fold →

You've
Been
Mugged!

MUG'EMS
by
CQ Products
www.cqproducts.com

You've
Been
Mugged!

MUG'EMS
by
CQ Products
www.cqproducts.com

Carrot Cake

Carrot Cake Mix
1 small egg
1 T. vegetable oil
2 T. orange juice with pulp
2 T. shredded carrots

Preheat oven to 350°. In a small bowl, place Carrot Cake Mix from bag. Add egg, vegetable oil, orange juice and shredded carrots and mix until well combined. Pour mixture into lightly greased mug. Bake in oven for 20 minutes. Enjoy!

Carrot Cake

Carrot Cake Mix
1 small egg
1 T. vegetable oil
2 T. orange juice with pulp
2 T. shredded carrots

Preheat oven to 350°. In a small bowl, place Carrot Cake Mix from bag. Add egg, vegetable oil, orange juice and shredded carrots and mix until well combined. Pour mixture into lightly greased mug. Bake in oven for 20 minutes. Enjoy!

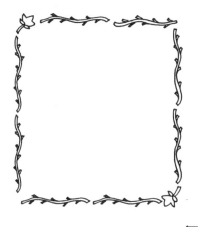

← fold →

You've
Been
Mugged!

You've
Been
Mugged!

MUG'EMS
by
CQ Products
www.cqproducts.com

MUG'EMS
by
CQ Products
www.cqproducts.com

Cinnamon Chocolate Cake Mix

4 T. flour
¾ tsp. baking powder
2½ T. sugar
1 T. cocoa powder
½ tsp. cinnamon
2 T. cinnamon baking chips

In a small bowl, combine above ingredients. Mix well and place in a sandwich-size ziplock bag and seal. Place sealed bag in a mug. Make sure the mug holds a volume of at least 1½ cups.

Decorate mug and attach a gift tag with the directions on how to prepare the cake.

Gift Tag Directions:
Cinnamon Chocolate Cake

Cinnamon Chocolate Cake Mix
3 T. shortening
1 small egg
3 T. milk
½ tsp. vanilla

Preheat oven to 350°. In a small bowl, place Cinnamon Chocolate Cake Mix from bag. Using a pastry blender, cut in shortening. Add egg, milk and vanilla and stir until thoroughly mixed, about 1 minute. Pour mixture into lightly greased mug. Bake in oven for 20 minutes. Enjoy!

Cinnamon Chocolate Cake

Cinnamon Chocolate Cake Mix
3 T. shortening
1 small egg
3 T. milk
½ tsp. vanilla

Preheat oven to 350°. In a small bowl, place Cinnamon Chocolate Cake Mix from bag. Using a pastry blender, cut in shortening. Add egg, milk and vanilla and stir until thoroughly mixed, about 1 minute. Pour mixture into lightly greased mug. Bake in oven for 20 minutes. Enjoy!

Cinnamon Chocolate Cake

Cinnamon Chocolate Cake Mix
3 T. shortening
1 small egg
3 T. milk
½ tsp. vanilla

Preheat oven to 350°. In a small bowl, place Cinnamon Chocolate Cake Mix from bag. Using a pastry blender, cut in shortening. Add egg, milk and vanilla and stir until thoroughly mixed, about 1 minute. Pour mixture into lightly greased mug. Bake in oven for 20 minutes. Enjoy!

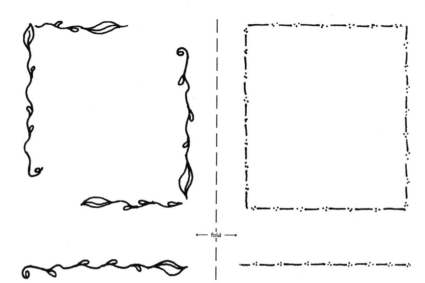

← fold →

You've
Been
Mugged!

You've
Been
Mugged!

MUG'EMS
by
CQ Products
www.cqproducts.com

MUG'EMS
by
CQ Products
www.cqproducts.com

Cinnamon Chocolate Cake

Cinnamon Chocolate Cake Mix
3 T. shortening
1 small egg
3 T. milk
½ tsp. vanilla

Preheat oven to 350°. In a small bowl, place Cinnamon Chocolate Cake Mix from bag. Using a pastry blender, cut in shortening. Add egg, milk and vanilla and stir until thoroughly mixed, about 1 minute. Pour mixture into lightly greased mug. Bake in oven for 20 minutes. Enjoy!

Cinnamon Chocolate Cake

Cinnamon Chocolate Cake Mix
3 T. shortening
1 small egg
3 T. milk
½ tsp. vanilla

Preheat oven to 350°. In a small bowl, place Cinnamon Chocolate Cake Mix from bag. Using a pastry blender, cut in shortening. Add egg, milk and vanilla and stir until thoroughly mixed, about 1 minute. Pour mixture into lightly greased mug. Bake in oven for 20 minutes. Enjoy!

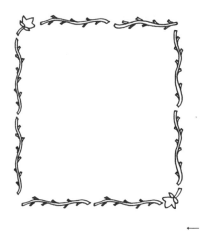

← fold →

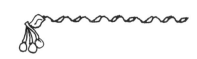

You've
Been
Mugged!

You've
Been
Mugged!

MUG'EMS
by
CQ Products
www.cqproducts.com

MUG'EMS
by
CQ Products
www.cqproducts.com

Gingerbread Cake Mix

4 T. flour
2 T. dark brown sugar
1 tsp. cocoa powder
¼ tsp. ground ginger
¼ tsp. baking powder
¼ tsp. baking soda
⅛ tsp. cinnamon
Pinch of nutmeg
Pinch of ground cloves

In a small bowl, combine above ingredients. Mix well and place in a sandwich-size ziplock bag and seal. Place sealed bag in a mug. Make sure the mug holds a volume of at least 1½ cups.

Decorate mug and attach a gift tag with the directions on how to prepare the cake.

Gift Tag Directions:
Gingerbread Cake

Gingerbread Cake Mix
2 T. molasses
1 small egg
2 T. warm water

Preheat oven to 350°. In a small bowl, place Gingerbread Cake Mix from bag. Add molasses, egg and warm water and blend until thoroughly mixed, about 1 minute. Pour mixture into lightly greased mug. Bake in oven for 20 minutes. Enjoy!

Gingerbread Cake

Gingerbread Cake Mix
2 T. molasses
1 small egg
2 T. warm water

Preheat oven to 350°. In a small bowl, place Gingerbread Cake Mix from bag. Add molasses, egg and warm water and blend until thoroughly mixed, about 1 minute. Pour mixture into lightly greased mug. Bake in oven for 20 minutes. Enjoy!

Gingerbread Cake

Gingerbread Cake Mix
2 T. molasses
1 small egg
2 T. warm water

Preheat oven to 350°. In a small bowl, place Gingerbread Cake Mix from bag. Add molasses, egg and warm water and blend until thoroughly mixed, about 1 minute. Pour mixture into lightly greased mug. Bake in oven for 20 minutes. Enjoy!

You've
Been
Mugged!

MUG'EMS
by
CQ Products
www.cqproducts.com

You've
Been
Mugged!

MUG'EMS
by
CQ Products
www.cqproducts.com

Gingerbread Cake

Gingerbread Cake Mix
2 T. molasses
1 small egg
2 T. warm water

Preheat oven to 350°. In a small bowl, place Gingerbread Cake Mix from bag. Add molasses, egg and warm water and blend until thoroughly mixed, about 1 minute. Pour mixture into lightly greased mug. Bake in oven for 20 minutes. Enjoy!

Gingerbread Cake

Gingerbread Cake Mix
2 T. molasses
1 small egg
2 T. warm water

Preheat oven to 350°. In a small bowl, place Gingerbread Cake Mix from bag. Add molasses, egg and warm water and blend until thoroughly mixed, about 1 minute. Pour mixture into lightly greased mug. Bake in oven for 20 minutes. Enjoy!

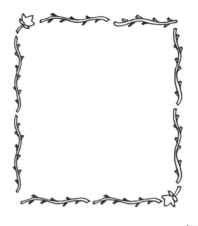

← fold →

You've
Been
Mugged!

You've
Been
Mugged!

MUG'EMS
by
CQ Products
www.cqproducts.com

MUG'EMS
by
CQ Products
www.cqproducts.com

Applesauce Cake Mix

1 tsp. cocoa powder
¼ C. flour
¼ tsp. cinnamon
¾ tsp. baking soda
3 T. sugar
1½ T. raisins
1 T. chopped walnuts or pecans

In a small bowl, combine above ingredients. Mix well and place in a sandwich-size ziplock bag and seal. Place sealed bag in a mug. Make sure the mug holds a volume of at least 1½ cups.

Decorate mug and attach a gift tag with the directions on how to prepare the cake.

Gift Tag Directions:
Applesauce Cake

Applesauce Cake Mix
2½ T. margarine, softened
1 small egg
⅓ C. applesauce

Preheat oven to 350°. In a small bowl, place Applesauce Cake Mix from bag. Add butter and mix until well combined. Add egg and applesauce and mix until well blended. Pour mixture into lightly greased mug. Bake in oven for 20 minutes. Enjoy!

Applesauce Cake

Applesauce Cake Mix
2½ T. margarine, softened
1 small egg
⅓ C. applesauce

Preheat oven to 350°. In a small bowl, place Applesauce Cake Mix from bag. Add butter and mix until well combined. Add egg and applesauce and mix until well blended. Pour mixture into lightly greased mug. Bake in oven for 20 minutes. Enjoy!

Applesauce Cake

Applesauce Cake Mix
2½ T. margarine, softened
1 small egg
⅓ C. applesauce

Preheat oven to 350°. In a small bowl, place Applesauce Cake Mix from bag. Add butter and mix until well combined. Add egg and applesauce and mix until well blended. Pour mixture into lightly greased mug. Bake in oven for 20 minutes. Enjoy!

fold

You've
Been
Mugged!

You've
Been
Mugged!

MUG'EMS
by
CQ Products
www.cqproducts.com

MUG'EMS
by
CQ Products
www.cqproducts.com

Applesauce Cake

Applesauce Cake Mix
2½ T. margarine, softened
1 small egg
⅓ C. applesauce

Preheat oven to 350°. In a small bowl, place Applesauce Cake Mix from bag. Add butter and mix until well combined. Add egg and applesauce and mix until well blended. Pour mixture into lightly greased mug. Bake in oven for 20 minutes. Enjoy!

Applesauce Cake

Applesauce Cake Mix
2½ T. margarine, softened
1 small egg
⅓ C. applesauce

Preheat oven to 350°. In a small bowl, place Applesauce Cake Mix from bag. Add butter and mix until well combined. Add egg and applesauce and mix until well blended. Pour mixture into lightly greased mug. Bake in oven for 20 minutes. Enjoy!

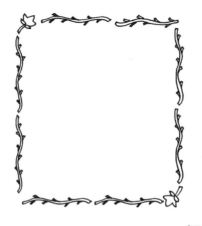

← fold →

You've
Been
Mugged!

You've
Been
Mugged!

MUG'EMS
by
CQ Products
www.cqproducts.com

MUG'EMS
by
CQ Products
www.cqproducts.com

Indian Pudding Mix

2 T. sugar
2 T. cornmeal
Pinch of nutmeg
Pinch of ground ginger

In a small bowl, combine above ingredients. Mix well and place in a sandwich-size ziplock bag and seal. Place sealed bag in a mug. Make sure the mug holds a volume of at least 1½ cups.

Decorate mug and attach a gift tag with the directions on how to prepare the pudding.

Gift Tag Directions:
Indian Pudding Mix

1 T. butter, melted
2 T. molasses
1 egg yolk
¾ C. whole milk
½ tsp. vanilla
Indian Pudding Mix

Preheat oven to 325°. In a small glass bowl, combine melted butter, molasses, egg yolk, milk and vanilla. Mix well and add Indian Pudding Mix from bag. Mix well and place mixture in microwave. Microwave on high for 2 minutes, until mixture is just simmering. Pour mixture into lightly greased mug. Bake in oven for 15 minutes. Enjoy!

Indian Pudding Mix

1 T. butter, melted
2 T. molasses
1 egg yolk
¾ C. whole milk
½ tsp. vanilla
Indian Pudding Mix

Preheat oven to 325°. In a small glass bowl, combine melted butter, molasses, egg yolk, milk and vanilla. Mix well and add Indian Pudding Mix from bag. Mix well and place mixture in microwave. Microwave on high for 2 minutes, until mixture is just simmering. Pour mixture into lightly greased mug. Bake in oven for 15 minutes. Enjoy!

Indian Pudding Mix

1 T. butter, melted
2 T. molasses
1 egg yolk
¾ C. whole milk
½ tsp. vanilla
Indian Pudding Mix

Preheat oven to 325°. In a small glass bowl, combine melted butter, molasses, egg yolk, milk and vanilla. Mix well and add Indian Pudding Mix from bag. Mix well and place mixture in microwave. Microwave on high for 2 minutes, until mixture is just simmering. Pour mixture into lightly greased mug. Bake in oven for 15 minutes. Enjoy!

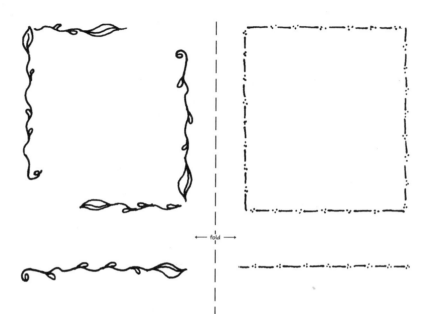

← fold →

You've
Been
Mugged!

MUG'EMS
by
CQ Products
www.cqproducts.com

You've
Been
Mugged!

MUG'EMS
by
CQ Products
www.cqproducts.com

Indian Pudding Mix

1 T. butter, melted
2 T. molasses
1 egg yolk
¾ C. whole milk
½ tsp. vanilla
Indian Pudding Mix

Preheat oven to 325°. In a small glass bowl, combine melted butter, molasses, egg yolk, milk and vanilla. Mix well and add Indian Pudding Mix from bag. Mix well and place mixture in microwave. Microwave on high for 2 minutes, until mixture is just simmering. Pour mixture into lightly greased mug. Bake in oven for 15 minutes. Enjoy!

Indian Pudding Mix

1 T. butter, melted
2 T. molasses
1 egg yolk
¾ C. whole milk
½ tsp. vanilla
Indian Pudding Mix

Preheat oven to 325°. In a small glass bowl, combine melted butter, molasses, egg yolk, milk and vanilla. Mix well and add Indian Pudding Mix from bag. Mix well and place mixture in microwave. Microwave on high for 2 minutes, until mixture is just simmering. Pour mixture into lightly greased mug. Bake in oven for 15 minutes. Enjoy!

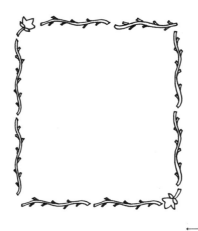

← fold →

You've
Been
Mugged!

You've
Been
Mugged!

MUG'EMS
by
CQ Products
www.cqproducts.com

MUG'EMS
by
CQ Products
www.cqproducts.com

Peanut Butter Cheesecake Mix

4 T. graham cracker crumbs
4 T. sugar, divided
¼ tsp. cinnamon, optional
2 T. miniature chocolate chips
1 tsp. flour

In a small bowl, combine graham cracker crumbs, 1 tablespoon sugar and cinnamon. Mix well and place in a small ziplock bag and seal. Place sealed bag in a mug. Make sure the mug holds a volume of at least 1½ cups. In a separate ziplock bag, place miniature chocolate chips, remaining 3 tablespoons sugar and flour. Place bag inside mug with other bag.

Decorate mug and attach a gift tag with the directions on how to prepare the cheesecake.

Gift Tag Directions:
Peanut Butter Cheesecake

2 T. melted butter
Peanut Butter Cheesecake Mix
4 oz. cream cheese, softened
1 egg yolk
¼ C. peanut butter
1 T. whole milk
½ tsp. vanilla

Preheat oven to 350°. To make crust, in a small bowl, combine melted butter and contents of bag containing graham cracker crumbs. Mix well and press mixture into the bottom and halfway up sides of lightly greased mug. Bake in oven for 6 to 8 minutes. Meanwhile, in a separate bowl, combine contents of remaining bag, cream cheese, egg yolk, peanut butter, whole milk and vanilla. Mix for 1 minute, until smooth. Allow crust to cool slightly and pour cream cheese mixture over crust in mug. Bake in oven for 20 minutes. Enjoy!

Peanut Butter Cheesecake

2 T. melted butter
Peanut Butter Cheesecake
   Mix
4 oz. cream cheese, softened
1 egg yolk
¼ C. peanut butter
1 T. whole milk
½ tsp. vanilla

Preheat oven to 350°. To make crust, in a small bowl, combine melted butter and contents of bag containing graham cracker crumbs. Mix well and press mixture into the bottom and halfway up sides of lightly greased mug. Bake in oven for 6 to 8 minutes. Meanwhile, in a separate bowl, combine contents of remaining bag, cream cheese, egg yolk, peanut butter, whole milk and vanilla. Mix for 1 minute, until smooth. Allow crust to cool slightly and pour cream cheese mixture over crust in mug. Bake in oven for 20 minutes. Enjoy!

Peanut Butter Cheesecake

2 T. melted butter
Peanut Butter Cheesecake
   Mix
4 oz. cream cheese, softened
1 egg yolk
¼ C. peanut butter
1 T. whole milk
½ tsp. vanilla

Preheat oven to 350°. To make crust, in a small bowl, combine melted butter and contents of bag containing graham cracker crumbs. Mix well and press mixture into the bottom and halfway up sides of lightly greased mug. Bake in oven for 6 to 8 minutes. Meanwhile, in a separate bowl, combine contents of remaining bag, cream cheese, egg yolk, peanut butter, whole milk and vanilla. Mix for 1 minute, until smooth. Allow crust to cool slightly and pour cream cheese mixture over crust in mug. Bake in oven for 20 minutes. Enjoy!

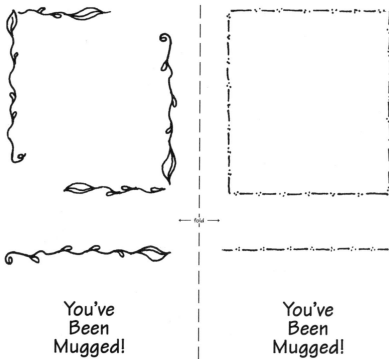

← fold →

You've
Been
Mugged!

MUG'EMS
by
CQ Products
www.cqproducts.com

You've
Been
Mugged!

MUG'EMS
by
CQ Products
www.cqproducts.com

Peanut Butter Cheesecake

2 T. melted butter
Peanut Butter Cheesecake
    Mix
4 oz. cream cheese, softened
1 egg yolk
¼ C. peanut butter
1 T. whole milk
½ tsp. vanilla

Preheat oven to 350°. To make crust, in a small bowl, combine melted butter and contents of bag containing graham cracker crumbs. Mix well and press mixture into the bottom and halfway up sides of lightly greased mug. Bake in oven for 6 to 8 minutes. Meanwhile, in a separate bowl, combine contents of remaining bag, cream cheese, egg yolk, peanut butter, whole milk and vanilla. Mix for 1 minute, until smooth. Allow crust to cool slightly and pour cream cheese mixture over crust in mug. Bake in oven for 20 minutes. Enjoy!

Peanut Butter Cheesecake

2 T. melted butter
Peanut Butter Cheesecake
    Mix
4 oz. cream cheese, softened
1 egg yolk
¼ C. peanut butter
1 T. whole milk
½ tsp. vanilla

Preheat oven to 350°. To make crust, in a small bowl, combine melted butter and contents of bag containing graham cracker crumbs. Mix well and press mixture into the bottom and halfway up sides of lightly greased mug. Bake in oven for 6 to 8 minutes. Meanwhile, in a separate bowl, combine contents of remaining bag, cream cheese, egg yolk, peanut butter, whole milk and vanilla. Mix for 1 minute, until smooth. Allow crust to cool slightly and pour cream cheese mixture over crust in mug. Bake in oven for 20 minutes. Enjoy!

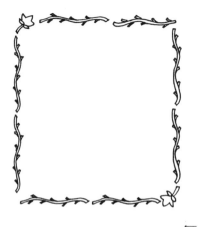

← fold →

You've
Been
Mugged!

You've
Been
Mugged!

MUG'EMS
by
CQ Products
www.cqproducts.com

MUG'EMS
by
CQ Products
www.cqproducts.com

Vanilla Coconut Dessert Mix

2 T. instant rice
1 (3 or 3¼ oz.) pkg. vanilla
    pudding mix
2 T. chopped dates
1 T. shredded coconut

In a small bowl, combine above ingredients. Mix well and place in a sandwich-size ziplock bag and seal. Place sealed bag in a mug. Make sure the mug holds a volume of at least 1½ cups.

Decorate mug and attach a gift tag with the directions on how to prepare the dessert.

Gift Tag Directions:
Vanilla Coconut Dessert

1 C. whole milk
Vanilla Coconut Dessert Mix

Place Vanilla Coconut Dessert Mix from bag in mug. In a small saucepan over medium low heat, bring whole milk just to a simmer. Pour simmering milk over ingredients in mug. Cover and let sit for 5 to 10 minutes. Stir slightly and let cool. Enjoy!

Vanilla Coconut Dessert

1 C. whole milk
Vanilla Coconut Dessert Mix

Place Vanilla Coconut Dessert Mix from bag in mug. In a small saucepan over medium low heat, bring whole milk just to a simmer. Pour simmering milk over ingredients in mug. Cover and let sit for 5 to 10 minutes. Stir slightly and let cool. Enjoy!

Vanilla Coconut Dessert

1 C. whole milk
Vanilla Coconut Dessert Mix

Place Vanilla Coconut Dessert Mix from bag in mug. In a small saucepan over medium low heat, bring whole milk just to a simmer. Pour simmering milk over ingredients in mug. Cover and let sit for 5 to 10 minutes. Stir slightly and let cool. Enjoy!

← fold →

You've
Been
Mugged!

You've
Been
Mugged!

MUG'EMS
by
CQ Products
www.cqproducts.com

MUG'EMS
by
CQ Products
www.cqproducts.com

Vanilla Coconut Dessert

1 C. whole milk
Vanilla Coconut Dessert Mix

Place Vanilla Coconut Dessert Mix from bag in mug. In a small saucepan over medium low heat, bring whole milk just to a simmer. Pour simmering milk over ingredients in mug. Cover and let sit for 5 to 10 minutes. Stir slightly and let cool. Enjoy!

Vanilla Coconut Dessert

1 C. whole milk
Vanilla Coconut Dessert Mix

Place Vanilla Coconut Dessert Mix from bag in mug. In a small saucepan over medium low heat, bring whole milk just to a simmer. Pour simmering milk over ingredients in mug. Cover and let sit for 5 to 10 minutes. Stir slightly and let cool. Enjoy!

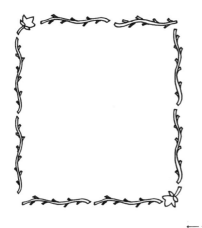

← fold →

You've
Been
Mugged!

You've
Been
Mugged!

MUG'EMS
by
CQ Products
www.cqproducts.com

MUG'EMS
by
CQ Products
www.cqproducts.com

Fruity Tapioca Mix

½ (3 oz.) pkg. tapioca pudding mix
1 T. currants
¼ C. miniature marshmallows
1 (4 oz.) can diced peaches in juice

In a small bowl, combine tapioca pudding mix and currants. Mix well and place in a small ziplock bag and seal. In a separate ziplock bag, place miniature marshmallows. Place can of diced peaches in mug and top with the two filled bags. Make sure the mug holds a volume of at least 1½ cups.

Decorate mug and attach a gift tag with the directions on how to prepare the tapioca.

Gift Tag Directions:
Fruity Tapioca

½ C. milk
Fruity Tapioca Mix

Place contents of bag containing currants in mug. Add peaches (along with juice) and mix well. Add milk and mix until thoroughly combined. Microwave on high until mixture begins to boil, about 3 minutes. Mixture should be thin. Remove from microwave and stir. Return to microwave for an additional 1 to 2 minutes, being careful mixture does not boil. Stir in miniature marshmallows. Cover and chill in refrigerator for 15 to 30 minutes. Enjoy!

Fruity Tapioca

½ C. milk
Fruity Tapioca Mix

Place contents of bag containing currants in mug. Add peaches (along with juice) and mix well. Add milk and mix until thoroughly combined. Microwave on high until mixture begins to boil, about 3 minutes. Mixture should be thin. Remove from microwave and stir. Return to microwave for an additional 1 to 2 minutes, being careful mixture does not boil. Stir in miniature marshmallows. Cover and chill in refrigerator for 15 to 30 minutes. Enjoy!

Fruity Tapioca

½ C. milk
Fruity Tapioca Mix

Place contents of bag containing currants in mug. Add peaches (along with juice) and mix well. Add milk and mix until thoroughly combined. Microwave on high until mixture begins to boil, about 3 minutes. Mixture should be thin. Remove from microwave and stir. Return to microwave for an additional 1 to 2 minutes, being careful mixture does not boil. Stir in miniature marshmallows. Cover and chill in refrigerator for 15 to 30 minutes. Enjoy!

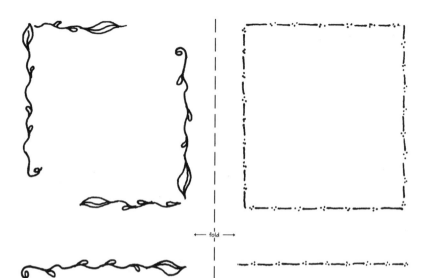

fold

You've
Been
Mugged!

You've
Been
Mugged!

MUG'EMS
by
CQ Products
www.cqproducts.com

MUG'EMS
by
CQ Products
www.cqproducts.com

Fruity Tapioca

½ C. milk
Fruity Tapioca Mix

Place contents of bag containing currants in mug. Add peaches (along with juice) and mix well. Add milk and mix until thoroughly combined. Microwave on high until mixture begins to boil, about 3 minutes. Mixture should be thin. Remove from microwave and stir. Return to microwave for an additional 1 to 2 minutes, being careful mixture does not boil. Stir in miniature marshmallows. Cover and chill in refrigerator for 15 to 30 minutes. Enjoy!

Fruity Tapioca

½ C. milk
Fruity Tapioca Mix

Place contents of bag containing currants in mug. Add peaches (along with juice) and mix well. Add milk and mix until thoroughly combined. Microwave on high until mixture begins to boil, about 3 minutes. Mixture should be thin. Remove from microwave and stir. Return to microwave for an additional 1 to 2 minutes, being careful mixture does not boil. Stir in miniature marshmallows. Cover and chill in refrigerator for 15 to 30 minutes. Enjoy!

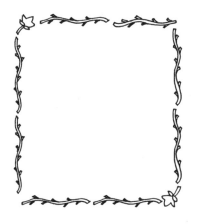

You've
Been
Mugged!

You've
Been
Mugged!

MUG'EMS
by
CQ Products
www.cqproducts.com

MUG'EMS
by
CQ Products
www.cqproducts.com

Granola Brown Betty Mix

3 T. sugar
1½ T. flour, divided
3 T. old fashioned oats
2 T. brown sugar
2 T. finely chopped walnuts
¼ tsp. cinnamon

In a small bowl, combine sugar and ½ tablespoon flour. Mix well and place in a small ziplock bag and seal. Place sealed bag in a mug. Make sure the mug holds a volume of at least 1½ cups. In a separate ziplock bag, place oats, brown sugar, finely chopped walnuts, cinnamon and remaining 1 tablespoon flour. Place bag inside mug with other bag.

Decorate mug and attach a gift tag with the directions on how to prepare the dessert.

Gift Tag Directions:
Granola Brown Betty

1 small pear
Granola Brown Betty Mix
3 T. butter, softened

Preheat oven to 350°. Peel, core and chop pear. In a small bowl, place contents of bag containing sugar and flour. Add chopped pear and toss until blended. Pour mixture into lightly greased mug. In a separate bowl, place contents of remaining bag. Using a pastry blender, cut in butter until mixture is crumbly. Place oats mixture over pear mixture in mug. Bake in oven for 20 minutes.

Granola Brown Betty

1 small pear
Granola Brown Betty Mix
3 T. butter, softened

Preheat oven to 350°. Peel, core and chop pear. In a small bowl, place contents of bag containing sugar and flour. Add chopped pear and toss until blended. Pour mixture into lightly greased mug. In a separate bowl, place contents of remaining bag. Using a pastry blender, cut in butter until mixture is crumbly. Place oats mixture over pear mixture in mug. Bake in oven for 20 minutes.

Granola Brown Betty

1 small pear
Granola Brown Betty Mix
3 T. butter, softened

Preheat oven to 350°. Peel, core and chop pear. In a small bowl, place contents of bag containing sugar and flour. Add chopped pear and toss until blended. Pour mixture into lightly greased mug. In a separate bowl, place contents of remaining bag. Using a pastry blender, cut in butter until mixture is crumbly. Place oats mixture over pear mixture in mug. Bake in oven for 20 minutes.

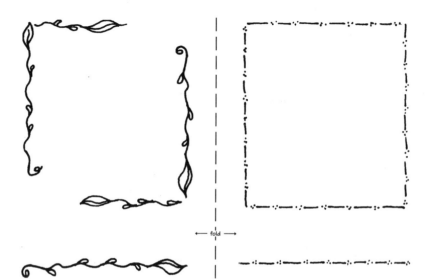

← fold →

You've
Been
Mugged!

MUG'EMS
by
CQ Products
www.cqproducts.com

You've
Been
Mugged!

MUG'EMS
by
CQ Products
www.cqproducts.com

Granola Brown Betty

1 small pear
Granola Brown Betty Mix
3 T. butter, softened

Preheat oven to 350°. Peel, core and chop pear. In a small bowl, place contents of bag containing sugar and flour. Add chopped pear and toss until blended. Pour mixture into lightly greased mug. In a separate bowl, place contents of remaining bag. Using a pastry blender, cut in butter until mixture is crumbly. Place oats mixture over pear mixture in mug. Bake in oven for 20 minutes.

Granola Brown Betty

1 small pear
Granola Brown Betty Mix
3 T. butter, softened

Preheat oven to 350°. Peel, core and chop pear. In a small bowl, place contents of bag containing sugar and flour. Add chopped pear and toss until blended. Pour mixture into lightly greased mug. In a separate bowl, place contents of remaining bag. Using a pastry blender, cut in butter until mixture is crumbly. Place oats mixture over pear mixture in mug. Bake in oven for 20 minutes.

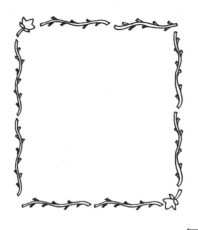

← fold →

You've
Been
Mugged!

You've
Been
Mugged!

MUG'EMS
by
CQ Products
www.cqproducts.com

MUG'EMS
by
CQ Products
www.cqproducts.com

Cherry Peach Cobbler Mix

¼ C. golden raisins
¼ C. dried cherries
4 T. sugar, divided
⅓ C. plus 2 tsp. flour, divided
½ tsp. baking powder
⅛ tsp. salt
1 (4 oz.) can diced peaches in juice

In a small bowl, combine golden raisins, dried cherries, 3 tablespoons sugar and 2 teaspoons flour. Mix well and place in a small ziplock bag and seal. In a separate ziplock bag, place remaining ⅓ cup flour, remaining 1 tablespoon sugar, baking powder and salt. Place can of diced peaches in a mug and top with the two filled bags. Make sure the mug holds a volume of at least 1½ cups.

Decorate mug and attach a gift tag with the directions on how to prepare the cobbler.

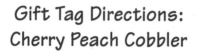

Gift Tag Directions:
Cherry Peach Cobbler

Cherry Peach Cobbler Mix
2 T. butter, softened
2 T. whole milk

Preheat oven to 350°. In a small bowl, place contents of bag containing dried cherries. Add peaches (along with juice) and mix well. Pour mixture into lightly greased mug. In a separate bowl, place contents of remaining bag. Using a pastry blender, cut in butter. Add milk and stir until well combined. On a lightly floured, flat surface, pat dough into a round crust. Place over fruit mixture in mug. Bake in oven for 20 to 25 minutes.

Cherry Peach Cobbler

Cherry Peach Cobbler Mix
2 T. butter, softened
2 T. whole milk

Preheat oven to 350°. In a small bowl, place contents of bag containing dried cherries. Add peaches (along with juice) and mix well. Pour mixture into lightly greased mug. In a separate bowl, place contents of remaining bag. Using a pastry blender, cut in butter. Add milk and stir until well combined. On a lightly floured, flat surface, pat dough into a round crust. Place over fruit mixture in mug. Bake in oven for 20 to 25 minutes.

Cherry Peach Cobbler

Cherry Peach Cobbler Mix
2 T. butter, softened
2 T. whole milk

Preheat oven to 350°. In a small bowl, place contents of bag containing dried cherries. Add peaches (along with juice) and mix well. Pour mixture into lightly greased mug. In a separate bowl, place contents of remaining bag. Using a pastry blender, cut in butter. Add milk and stir until well combined. On a lightly floured, flat surface, pat dough into a round crust. Place over fruit mixture in mug. Bake in oven for 20 to 25 minutes.

You've
Been
Mugged!

MUG'EMS
by
CQ Products
www.cqproducts.com

You've
Been
Mugged!

MUG'EMS
by
CQ Products
www.cqproducts.com

← fold →

Cherry Peach Cobbler

Cherry Peach Cobbler Mix
2 T. butter, softened
2 T. whole milk

Preheat oven to 350°. In a small bowl, place contents of bag containing dried cherries. Add peaches (along with juice) and mix well. Pour mixture into lightly greased mug. In a separate bowl, place contents of remaining bag. Using a pastry blender, cut in butter. Add milk and stir until well combined. On a lightly floured, flat surface, pat dough into a round crust. Place over fruit mixture in mug. Bake in oven for 20 to 25 minutes.

Cherry Peach Cobbler

Cherry Peach Cobbler Mix
2 T. butter, softened
2 T. whole milk

Preheat oven to 350°. In a small bowl, place contents of bag containing dried cherries. Add peaches (along with juice) and mix well. Pour mixture into lightly greased mug. In a separate bowl, place contents of remaining bag. Using a pastry blender, cut in butter. Add milk and stir until well combined. On a lightly floured, flat surface, pat dough into a round crust. Place over fruit mixture in mug. Bake in oven for 20 to 25 minutes.

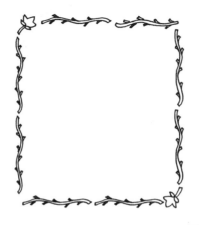

← fold →

You've
Been
Mugged!

You've
Been
Mugged!

MUG'EMS
by
CQ Products
www.cqproducts.com

MUG'EMS
by
CQ Products
www.cqproducts.com

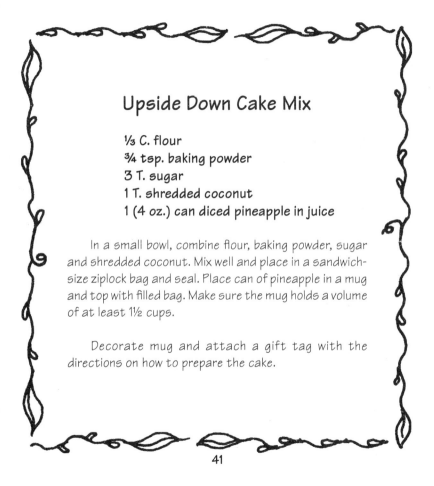

Upside Down Cake Mix

⅓ C. flour
¾ tsp. baking powder
3 T. sugar
1 T. shredded coconut
1 (4 oz.) can diced pineapple in juice

In a small bowl, combine flour, baking powder, sugar and shredded coconut. Mix well and place in a sandwich-size ziplock bag and seal. Place can of pineapple in a mug and top with filled bag. Make sure the mug holds a volume of at least 1½ cups.

Decorate mug and attach a gift tag with the directions on how to prepare the cake.

Gift Tag Directions:
Upside Down Cake

Upside Down Cake Mix
2½ T. shortening
1 small egg
3 T. milk
½ tsp. vanilla
½ T. butter, melted
1 T. brown sugar
3 or 4 maraschino cherries

Preheat oven to 350°. In a small bowl, place Upside Down Cake Mix from bag. Using a pastry blender, cut in shortening. Add egg, milk and vanilla and mix until thoroughly combined, about 1 minute. Place melted butter in mug and sprinkle with brown sugar. Place maraschino cherries and drained pineapple from can in mug over brown sugar. Pour cake batter over fruit in mug. Bake in oven for 15 to 20 minutes.

Upside Down Cake

Upside Down Cake Mix
2½ T. shortening
1 small egg
3 T. milk
½ tsp. vanilla
½ T. butter, melted
1 T. brown sugar
3 or 4 maraschino cherries

Preheat oven to 350°. In a small bowl, place Upside Down Cake Mix from bag. Using a pastry blender, cut in shortening. Add egg, milk and vanilla and mix until thoroughly combined, about 1 minute. Place melted butter in mug and sprinkle with brown sugar. Place maraschino cherries and drained pineapple from can in mug over brown sugar. Pour cake batter over fruit in mug. Bake in oven for 15 to 20 minutes.

Upside Down Cake

Upside Down Cake Mix
2½ T. shortening
1 small egg
3 T. milk
½ tsp. vanilla
½ T. butter, melted
1 T. brown sugar
3 or 4 maraschino cherries

Preheat oven to 350°. In a small bowl, place Upside Down Cake Mix from bag. Using a pastry blender, cut in shortening. Add egg, milk and vanilla and mix until thoroughly combined, about 1 minute. Place melted butter in mug and sprinkle with brown sugar. Place maraschino cherries and drained pineapple from can in mug over brown sugar. Pour cake batter over fruit in mug. Bake in oven for 15 to 20 minutes.

You've
Been
Mugged!

MUG'EMS
by
CQ Products
www.cqproducts.com

You've
Been
Mugged!

MUG'EMS
by
CQ Products
www.cqproducts.com

Upside Down Cake

Upside Down Cake Mix
2½ T. shortening
1 small egg
3 T. milk
½ tsp. vanilla
½ T. butter, melted
1 T. brown sugar
3 or 4 maraschino cherries

Preheat oven to 350°. In a small bowl, place Upside Down Cake Mix from bag. Using a pastry blender, cut in shortening. Add egg, milk and vanilla and mix until thoroughly combined, about 1 minute. Place melted butter in mug and sprinkle with brown sugar. Place maraschino cherries and drained pineapple from can in mug over brown sugar. Pour cake batter over fruit in mug. Bake in oven for 15 to 20 minutes.

Upside Down Cake

Upside Down Cake Mix
2½ T. shortening
1 small egg
3 T. milk
½ tsp. vanilla
½ T. butter, melted
1 T. brown sugar
3 or 4 maraschino cherries

Preheat oven to 350°. In a small bowl, place Upside Down Cake Mix from bag. Using a pastry blender, cut in shortening. Add egg, milk and vanilla and mix until thoroughly combined, about 1 minute. Place melted butter in mug and sprinkle with brown sugar. Place maraschino cherries and drained pineapple from can in mug over brown sugar. Pour cake batter over fruit in mug. Bake in oven for 15 to 20 minutes.

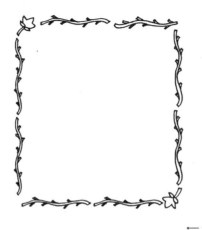

← *fold* →

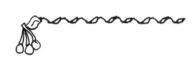

You've
Been
Mugged!

You've
Been
Mugged!

MUG'EMS
by
CQ Products
www.cqproducts.com

MUG'EMS
by
CQ Products
www.cqproducts.com

Index

Almond Cheesecake Mix..1

Apple Crisp Mix...15

Applesauce Cake Mix..27

Baked Custard Mix..3

Bread Pudding Mix...19

Carrot Cake Mix...21

Cherry Peach Cobbler Mix..39

Chocolate Cakelette Mix...17

Chocolate Chip Blondie Mix...9

Cinnamon Chocolate Cake Mix......................................23

Fruity Tapioca Mix...35

Fudge Brownie Mix..5

Gingerbread Cake Mix..25

Granola Brown Betty Mix..37

Indian Pudding Mix..29

Mocha Pudding Mix..7

Peanut Butter Cheesecake Mix.....................................31

Rice Pudding Mix...11

Shoofly Pie Mix...13

Upside Down Cake Mix...41

Vanilla Coconut Dessert Mix...33

Tips on Preparing & Decorating:

- Holiday themed food-safe bags, normally found at your local craft store, add a nice touch to your gift.

- It is often easier to place the open bag in the mug first. Then pour the ingredients into the open bag and seal. If needed, use a thin paper plate as a funnel.

- Before decorating the bag with ribbon, raffia or a fabric strip, first close the bag with a rubber band or twist tie.

- Add your personalized greeting to one side of the gift tag then fold in half. Punch a hole into the corner of the tag and use ribbon, raffia, twine, lace or a fabric strip to attach the tag to the mug.

- Mug 'Ems make great gifts for Mother's Day, birthdays, holidays or a sick friend. Accessorize the gift by attaching a small gift such as a stirring spoon, fork or hot pad to the mug.